JESUS IS MY SPECIAL FRIEND

by Susan S. Balika
illustrated by Craig Boldman

Ninth Printing, 1989
Library of Congress Catalog Card No. 81-86702

I have a friend.
His name is Jimmy.

Jimmy and I like to talk together.
We wonder where clouds come from.

We plan rocket trips to the moon.
We laugh about the way pudding
feels in our mouths.

But sometimes Jimmy goes shopping
   with his mother.
Sometimes he goes to visit his grandparents.

When we can't be together, I feel lonely.

I had a friend.
Her name was Jamie.

We liked to look at books
and tell stories about the pictures.

We liked to color with bright crayons.
Sometimes our mothers taped our drawings
onto the refrigerator.

One day a moving van came.
The moving men put Jamie's books
and crayons into brown boxes.

They took down her swing set.
Jamie moved away to another city.
I miss her.

I have another friend.
His name is David.
David and I like to play games together.

We build roads in the sand
and make garages from blocks.

We pretend that David is the mechanic
and I am a race-car driver.

Sometimes we fight.
We get angry with each other.
David takes his big, yellow dump truck
and goes home.

That makes me feel sad inside.
It is hard to say "I'm sorry."

But I have a very special Friend.
He never makes me feel lonely.
He never moves away.
He never goes home because He is angry with me.
He is always with me, even though I can't see Him.

He is with me when I lie on my back
in the tickly green grass
and look up at the clouds.

He is with me when I toss leaves high in the air
and jump in the falling colors.

He is with me when I whoosh down the hill
in the crunchy snow.
He is with me because He wants to be with me.

If I do something wrong,
He lets me say "I'm sorry."

He even likes me when I do not like myself.

And He likes all my friends.
He likes you as much as He likes me.
He loves you as much as He loves me.
My special Friend is Jesus.

Do you know my special Friend?
Do you know Jesus?